AMAZING FEATS OF

CIVIL ENGINEERING

Essential Library

An Imprint of Abdo Publishing | www.abdopublishing.com

AMAZING FEATS OF

CIVIL ENGINEERING

by L. E. Carmichael

Content Consultant

David A. Lange
Professor
Department of Civil & Environmental Engineering
University of Illinois at Urbana-Champaign

www.abdopublishing.com

Published by Abdo Publishing, a division of ABDO, PO Box 398166, Minneapolis, Minnesota 55439. Copyright © 2015 by Abdo Consulting Group, Inc. International copyrights reserved in all countries. No part of this book may be reproduced in any form without written permission from the publisher. Essential Library™ is a trademark and logo of Abdo Publishing.

Printed in the United States of America, North Mankato, Minnesota
042014
092014

THIS BOOK CONTAINS
RECYCLED MATERIALS

Cover Photo: Steve Buckley/Shutterstock Images
Interior Photos: Steve Buckley/Shutterstock Images, 2; Irina Schmidt/Shutterstock Images, 7; Kamran Jebreili/AP Images, 9, 47, 50, 59; Rigucci/Shutterstock Images, 12; Ben Chrisman/The Daily Times/AP Images, 13; Shutterstock Images, 17, 52, 63; Matteo Gabrieli/Shutterstock Images, 19; Georgios Kollidas/Shutterstock Images, 23; Iain Masterton/age fotostock/SuperStock, 25; Quint & Lox Limited/SuperStock, 27; V. J. Matthew/Shutterstock Images, 31; Barrett & MacKay/All Canada Photos/SuperStock, 32; Red Line Editorial, 35; Bouly, Strait Crossing Development Inc./AP Images, 37; Barrett & MacKay/Glow Images, 40, 43; Nasser Younes/AFP/Getty Images, 54; Ilona Ignatova/Shutterstock Images, 56; Alisdair Miller/Solent News/Rex/AP Images, 64; North Wind Picture Archives, 67, 78; AP Images, 70, 72; Tomas van Houtryve/AP Images, 75; Arnulfo Franco/AP Images, 81, 87; Eduardo Verdugo/AP Images, 83; Ritu Manoj Jethani/Shutterstock Images, 89; NASA, 92; Vincent Callebaut/Solent New/Rex/AP Images, 95; Pat Christman/The Mankato Free Press/AP Images, 97

Editor: Arnold Ringstad
Series Designer: Becky Daum

Library of Congress Control Number: 2014932575

Cataloging-in-Publication Data

Carmichael, L. E.
  Amazing feats of civil engineering / L. E. Carmichael.
   p. cm. -- (Great achievements in engineering)
Includes index.
ISBN 978-1-62403-427-5
1. Civil engineering--Juvenile literature. 2. Structural engineering--Juvenile literature.   I. Title.
624--dc23

2014932575

Cover: The Golden Gate Bridge in San Francisco, California, is one of the world's most iconic structures.

CONTENTS

CHAPTER 1

WHAT IS CIVIL ENGINEERING?

Rising from the desert in the heart of the Middle Eastern city of Dubai is the Burj Khalifa, the tallest building ever constructed. On such a record-breaking project, everything has to be right—from the foundation supporting the tower to the glass and steel cladding separating its interior spaces from the external environment.

The outer covering, or curtain wall, would cost $100 million all by itself.[1] Eric Tomich, civil engineer and technical director on the project, was not willing to spend that kind of money without proof the new system would work. "If you erected a curtain wall," he said, "and you didn't find out how it had an inherent design flaw like a leak or

The Burj Khalifa stands more than a half mile (0.8 km) high.

something, until after [the building] was occupied and the first storm came. . . . It's unthinkable."[2]

To ensure the cladding could withstand Dubai's punishing climate, Tomich partnered with a corporation that had expertise in testing curtain walls. The team needed to know the system would survive earthquakes, extreme temperatures, and wind forces, all without allowing air or water to penetrate the building. "We try to put everything that mother nature would throw at the building into these tests," Tomich said.[3] At first, the team was unsure of how to simulate these conditions.

Engineers came up with an innovative solution—an airplane engine. The engine's propellers flung water against the test wall while generating high wind speeds. On the inner side of the test panels, everything stayed dry and airtight. With the cladding design validated, construction crews could now give the Burj Khalifa its skin.

THE BUILT ENVIRONMENT

Buildings, ranging from the megatall Burj Khalifa to a simple two-story apartment block, are just one example of civil engineering. Civil engineers are responsible for infrastructure, the constructed environments that make up and connect modern civilizations. Infrastructure includes the places where people live, work, and travel. Civil engineers build tunnels, bridges,

The Burj Khalifa's high-tech outer surface makes it possible for visitors to safely enjoy a meal more than 1,300 feet (400 m) above the ground.

dams, roads, railways, canals, and airports. They design water supply and treatment facilities, waste management and recycling plants, and communication and energy grids.

Infrastructure is the reason lights turn on with the flick of a switch and fresh, pure water pours from taps. It allows kids to safely walk to school

ENGINEERS, WATER, AND HEALTH

As recently as a century ago, sickness from contaminated water was a leading cause of death in the United States. Lewis Thomas, a dean of the Yale School of Medicine in the 1970s, once said "the greatest advances in improving human health were the development of clean drinking water and sewage systems. So, we owe our health as much to civil engineering as we do biology."[5]

Worldwide, polluted water still affects the health of hundreds of millions of people. "There are places in the world," said engineer Margaret Layne, "where a high percentage of children die before the age of five from waterborne diseases that haven't been seen in [the United States] for 150 years. That is certainly an area in which civil engineers have an opportunity to exert a significant impact on the quality of life."[6]

on sidewalks, and it makes it possible for Canadians to buy bananas in the dead of winter. According to Margaret Layne, former president of the Society of Women Engineers, "Civil engineers are the engineers who work on things that most directly affect our quality of life and things that can be shown to really have direct impact on improving life for other people."[4]

Many of civil engineering's greatest accomplishments function in the backdrop of daily life, going unnoticed unless they stop working. Others, however, dominate both landscapes and imaginations. Icons such as the

Eiffel Tower and the Golden Gate Bridge were designed and constructed by civil engineers.

A WORLD OF POSSIBILITIES

Depending on their interests, civil engineers can pursue a wide range of specialties. The work of environmental engineers includes protecting the natural environment and ensuring public health. Closely related are water resource engineers, who handle the safety of drinking water. Flooding and hydroelectric power production are also concerns of water resource engineers.

Transportation engineering focuses on the movement of people and products from place to place. Transportation specialists may work closely with urban planning engineers, who optimize street patterns and traffic flow within cities.

Structural engineers select construction materials and methods to ensure buildings can support their own weight and withstand external forces such as snow, waves, or wind. Strong

THE GOLDEN GATE BRIDGE

The Golden Gate Bridge, completed in 1937, is among the most famous products of civil engineering. Connecting San Francisco, California, and neighboring Marin County over San Francisco Bay, the bridge's iconic design and red color are known worldwide. The American Society of Civil Engineers declared it one of the seven wonders of the modern world.

Modern infrastructure gives people safe places to live and work and efficient ways to move from place to place.

foundations are key to structural stability, and geotechnical engineers focus on the behavior of rock and soil at the bases of structures during and after construction. Seismic engineers take this one step further by finding ways to keep structures intact during earthquakes. Construction engineers oversee all these specialists. They are responsible for designing, planning, and managing infrastructure projects from start to finish.

AN ENGINEER'S LIFE

Successful civil engineers have strong math, science, and problem-solving skills. They are creative, open-minded, and willing to think outside the box. Confidence, curiosity, and persistence are also helpful qualities.

Completing large infrastructure projects requires leadership and teamwork. Civil engineers must collaborate with one another and with architects, tradespeople, and engineers from other disciplines, such as mechanical or electrical engineering. Because the structures and systems they design are used by ordinary people, civil engineers must also consult and cooperate with the public. The ability to explain complex technical

Construction engineers are sometimes responsible for explaining major projects to public officials.

LIFELONG LEARNING

Innovations in civil engineering occur every day, so engineers must commit to lifelong learning. Engineer Christopher Pinto believes keeping up with these new developments is not only important, but exciting. In 2002, he said:

If you learned everything there is to know about building any structure on earth in school, you'd be in school forever . . . by the time you finished you'd have no desire to go out and do any of it. Part of the fun about being a structural engineer and what I do is learning something new every day.[10]

information in a clear way is critical. Many working engineers say communication skills are often more important to their daily success than the technical knowledge they acquired during their education.

Civil engineers hold the safety of the public in their hands. If dams burst or buildings collapse, people could be injured or killed. This responsibility may be part of the reason engineers earn high salaries. In 2012, they earned a median salary of $79,340 per year, compared to $34,750 across all careers.[7]

Of the 1.6 million engineers in the United States, more are civil engineers than any other type.[8] In 2012, 272,900 people were employed as civil engineers, and the US Bureau of Labor Statistics predicted more than 50,000 additional jobs would be added by the year 2022.[9]

Many civil engineers, however, feel the opportunity to improve people's lives is more

MAKING THE GRADE

The American Society of Civil Engineers issued its first report on US infrastructure in 1998. The report evaluates infrastructure types using eight criteria—including condition, public safety, and future need—and assigns a letter grade from A to F. It also includes recommendations for improving infrastructure quality. In 2013, the average grade for US infrastructure was a D+.

The group's president, Gregory E. DiLoreto, said, "Many of our roads, bridges, water systems, and our national electric grid were put into place over 50 years ago, and these systems are simply overwhelmed or worn out."[12] Experts estimate getting to a B grade across all infrastructure categories would require an investment of at least $2.2 trillion.[13]

important than high salaries or job security. Civil engineer and thirty-first US president Herbert Hoover said:

It is a great profession. There is the satisfaction of watching a figment of the imagination emerge through the aid of science to a plan on paper. Then it moves to realization in stone or metal or energy. Then it brings jobs and homes to men. Then it elevates the standards of living and adds to the comforts of life. That is the engineer's high privilege.[11]

CHAPTER 2

BUILDING A PROFESSION

The words *engineer* and *ingenious* come from the Latin *gignere*, meaning "to create."[1] The oldest branch of engineering, civil engineering began during the Neolithic Revolution approximately 10,000 years ago when the development of agriculture allowed people to form permanent settlements for the first time. Key innovations such as dams and paved roads seem to have been invented independently in several different places as early engineers found common solutions to shared problems.

Pyramids were among the largest engineering projects in the ancient world.

Imhotep, builder of Egypt's Step Pyramid, is the earliest engineer known by name. The Egyptian pyramids were among the first structures to be built of stone rather than wood or mud brick. Approximately 4,500 years old and originally 481 feet (147 m) tall, the Great Pyramid of Giza was the world's tallest building for more than 4,000 years. Covering 13 acres (5 ha) at the base, it is within one inch (2.54 cm) of being perfectly level. The more than 2 million blocks of limestone and granite used in its construction weigh between two and six short tons (1.8 and 5.4 metric tons) each. American civil engineer Craig B. Smith says,

> Its builders were remarkable. They had no pulleys, no wheels, no iron tools, no compasses—just crude chisels, saws, hammers, and drills made of copper, wood, and stone—and yet they flawlessly designed, sited, and erected this structure of precise geometric configuration and complex construction on an astonishing scale.[2]

The Romans were also accomplished engineers of the ancient world. Indeed, the oldest surviving book about engineering, *De Architectura*, was written by Roman engineer Vitruvius in the first century CE. He believed every structure should be durable, useful, and beautiful. The Roman aqueducts, built over a period of 500 years beginning in 313 BCE, certainly fit this description. Before their construction, cities had to be built near supplies of freshwater. The invention of these pipelines and

Portions of Rome's ancient aqueducts still stand today.

channels allowed water to be transported from springs in the countryside to city centers around the Roman Empire. Built of stone and lined with an early form of concrete, aqueducts were designed to take advantage of gravity by running downhill wherever possible.

Totaling hundreds of miles in length, 11 aqueducts served the capital city. The system delivered 200 gallons (750 L) for each of Rome's citizens every day.[3] Sextus Julius Frontinus, named Rome's water commissioner in 97 CE, called the aqueducts "indispensable" compared to "the idle pyramids or the useless, though famous, works of the Greeks."[4]

MEDIEVAL ENGINEERING

During the Middle Ages, advances in civil engineering centered around cathedrals. Often taking centuries to build, these vast churches required medieval builders to find new ways of supporting weight.

Thousands of years earlier, in the 400s BCE, Greek engineers had used vertical columns to support horizontal roof beams in structures such as the Parthenon. The longer the span between the columns, the more likely the beam would buckle under its own weight. For aqueducts and other projects, the Romans later developed semicircular arches, which used wedge-shaped rocks to create a curved span between the supports. This channeled the downward force of gravity laterally and then downward through supporting columns.

However, as cathedral engineers constructed taller walls and higher arches, they encountered a problem. The lateral forces moving through the arches became so strong they caused the walls to buckle outward.

SCIENCE AND ENGINEERING

Aerospace engineer Theodore von Kármán once said, "A scientist studies what is; an engineer creates what never was."[5] In other words, scientists work to understand the world around them, while engineers design and build entirely new environments. In truth, research scientists are a powerful addition to an engineer's team, especially on projects that push the boundaries of past experience. "There is a blurring of the boundaries between science and engineering," according to G. Wayne Clough, an award-winning geotechnical engineer. "And for good reason: the problems of today can't be solved by an engineer or a scientist; we've got to be working together."[6]

The invention of the buttress solved this problem. Built outside the wall of the church in line with its interior columns, buttresses had two parts: a half arch connecting to the wall and a vertical pier for support. Now the lateral forces from the interior arch could be channeled through the buttress and into the ground, allowing churches to reach greater heights than ever before.

AN ENGINEERING REVOLUTION

Medieval engineers did not have computers. Instead, they relied on instinct and experience—both their own and that of older master builders.

WOMEN IN CIVIL ENGINEERING

In 1930, there were 256,078 engineers in the United States. Only 18 were women.[7] By 2012, the percentage of working female civil engineers had risen to just 9.7 percent.[8] Minority women are the smallest demographic group of all.

Girls are just as likely as boys to enjoy math and science in high school, but many more boys pursue engineering. Professor of engineering Peggy Johnson sees this as a serious problem. "Not only does the profession need more qualified civil engineers," she says, "it needs a diverse pool of engineers to solve the vast array of highly complex, global problems that humanity faces now and in the future."[9]

Sarah Buck, first female president of the United Kingdom's Institution of Structural Engineers, agrees: "Girls need to know that the construction industry is not a male prerogative, and that if they are interested in structures and the built environment, then there is a rewarding career awaiting them."[10]

They also did not think of themselves as engineers. They were carpenters, toolmakers, stonemasons, and tradespeople.

Engineering as a recognized profession began in France in the 1700s with the establishment of the first engineering schools and textbooks. Professional societies developed, giving working engineers a place to meet, share their knowledge, and discuss the challenges they faced. One of these, the Society of Civil Engineers, was formed by John Smeaton in 1771. Smeaton built lighthouses, bridges, roads, and windmills throughout England and Scotland. He also coined the term *civil engineer* to distinguish infrastructure projects from the work of military engineers. In 1828, British engineer Thomas Tredgold provided the first official job

One of Smeaton's major projects was the Eddystone Lighthouse in England.

ENGINEERING IN THE DIGITAL AGE

Computers have had more impact on today's engineering than any other development. Just a few decades ago, engineers designed by hand, using slide rules for calculations. Today, three-dimensional design programs help engineers visualize structures and predict how they will behave under real-world conditions. New programs that include time as a variable can model planning and construction phases as well as changes over a structure's life-span. While they are powerful tools, computers cannot replace training and experience. Before trusting a program's output, engineers must always consider whether the answer makes structural sense.

description: "Civil engineering is the art of directing the great sources of power in nature for the use and convenience of man."[11]

Smeaton and Tredgold worked during the Industrial Revolution, a period of rapid urbanization. By 1900, a large majority of England's population lived in cities. Dense urban living conditions created new problems, and innovations in structural, transportation, and water resource engineering quickly followed. Iron began replacing stone as a building material, and engineers began new experiments with concrete. Advances in civil engineering during this period had a huge impact on the way people lived, worked, and got around.

Today, engineers plan structures on computers instead of paper, and they construct them from revolutionary new materials. Their mission remains the same, however. "Civil engineering knows no boundaries of time or place," says Amar Bhogal of the United Kingdom's Institution of Civil Engineers. "One can take great pride in the achievements of our profession, which are very much the landmarks of the development of humankind. Society relies upon us for all that it takes for granted and aspires to—clean water, power, transport and communications—for a decent quality of life."[12]

Computers and tablets are becoming an integral part of any civil engineer's toolbox.

CHAPTER 3

A FIXED LINK

Separated from mainland Canada by the Northumberland Strait, Prince Edward Island is best known as the setting of L. M. Montgomery's novel *Anne of Green Gables*. The island became a Canadian province on July 1, 1873, on the condition that the federal government would maintain a "continuous means of communication" between the island and the mainland. The strait is approximately eight miles (13 km) wide at its narrowest point, making this communication slow in the first decades after the island became a province.[1]

Crossing the Northumberland Strait was treacherous before the construction of a bridge.

DEADLY CROSSINGS

Until 1917, islanders crossed the wintery strait using iceboats. Fitted with runners, these boats could be hauled out at the edge of open water and dragged across ice floes. Male passengers paid a reduced fare if they agreed to help push.

On Saturday March 10, 1855, four crew members, three passengers, and a mail bundle began the crossing from New Brunswick to Prince Edward Island. They were only a few miles from arrival when a blizzard struck, pushing the ice they floated on farther from shore. By the time the men reached help Tuesday morning, all were badly frostbitten and one had died of exposure.

In winter, most of the strait is covered in ice, seriously impeding boat-based communication. It was not until 1917 that icebreakers could consistently make the crossing, a journey lasting between 45 and 60 minutes. Some wondered, however, if there was a better solution.

The first proposal to connect the island to the mainland, using a tunnel, was made in 1885 and soon dismissed. One hundred years later, three engineering firms sent the Canadian government new plans for a bridge over the strait. Politicians and the public alike were intrigued. The planned structure became known to residents of Prince Edward Island as the fixed link, referring to the general term for a permanent structure connecting two areas separated by a body of water. Its official name was Confederation Bridge.

PROTECTING THE ECOSYSTEM

Public Works Canada's document listing environmental requirements for Confederation Bridge was 104 pages long. As Copthorne Macdonald, author of *Bridging the Strait* put it, "Any contractor who focused only on steel and concrete and didn't [care] about the environment was not going to [build this bridge]."[2]

Despite the builders' willingness to meet these requirements, a protest group called Friends of the Island sued the Canadian government to prevent construction. Concerns ranged from impact on fisheries and migratory birds to increased traffic through the national wildlife area in Cape Jourimain. Judges ruled in favor of the project, however, and commended the contractor's thoroughness in incorporating environmental protection into its plans.

A TALL ORDER

Paul Giannelia, a civil engineer based in Alberta, Canada, had never built anything larger than the speed skating oval in Calgary, Alberta. But when the government agency Public Works Canada (PWC) called for official proposals in 1987 for an enormous bridge over the Northumberland Strait, he knew he wanted to build it.

Billion-dollar projects draw a lot of interest, so winning the contract would not be easy. In addition to engineers, Giannelia needed scientists on his team specializing in ice, wind, and even the ergonomics of driving.

SAFE DRIVING

Long, straight roads can have a hypnotic effect on drivers, making them less alert to potential hazards. To increase the safety of Confederation Bridge, engineers designed it with a gentle, S-shaped curve, forcing drivers to pay more attention. The idea came from Robert Dewar, a professor at the University of Calgary who specialized in the ergonomics of driving. Some members of Giannelia's team believed going beyond engineering to consider the drivability of their design helped them win the bridge contract.

Giannelia's plans called for a sturdy, functional design.

"We had to have the best technical solution," he said. "That was the only way that we could beat the kind of competition we were up against."[3]

Competition was not the only challenge Giannelia faced. PWC insisted on a significantly higher safety rating than the one specified for ordinary North American highway bridges. It also wanted a bridge that would last 100 years, double the life-span of bridges built in more temperate environments. To make matters worse, many residents of Prince Edward Island voted against the project. Their reasons ranged from environmental impacts to the loss of their island identity.

"The ongoing challenge for me was dealing with all the negativity," Giannelia remembered. "The biggest challenge, at the end of the day, was to make believers of the bystanders, the people in the middle, and the people on your own team."[4]

The huge volumes of ice that develop in the Northumberland Strait presented special challenges to the designers of Confederation Bridge.

After years of proposals, reviews, and even lawsuits meant to block the project, Giannelia won the competition. His group Strait Crossing Inc. (SCI) signed the contract to build Confederation Bridge in 1994. Connecting Cape Jourimain, New Brunswick, and Borden, Prince Edward Island, the bridge would cross the Northumberland Strait at its narrowest point. At eight miles (13 km) long, it would be the longest bridge over ice-covered water in the world.[5]

OVERCOMING ICE

Because a project of this nature had never been attempted, SCI's engineers had no established guidelines or experience to draw on.

ENGINEERING FOR MELTING

In addition to the impact of ice on the bridge, SCI had to account for the bridge's impact on ice. If the structure caused ice jamming or delayed spring melting, the changes could harm agriculture and lobster fishing.

Before the bridge was built, the last major melting typically occurred between April 2 and May 31. Thomas Brown, structural engineer and ice specialist, used 20 years of ice records and climate information to predict the structure's effect on the melting date. Based on early results, SCI increased the distance between neighboring bridge piers, reducing the risk of jams. This revised design should delay melting by no more than two days once a century.

Instead, they had to work from basic bridge-building principles, taking into account the forces exerted on the bridge by everyday traffic and the environment. These forces, called loads, included vehicles on the bridge deck, hurricanes, earthquakes, and even collisions with ships.

Ice loads would be the bridge's biggest threat. Ice forms along the coastlines of the strait in December and covers open water by January. Winds and tides push the floes back and forth. When they collide, floes combine to form ridges. Their bottoms are deep enough to scour the seabed, and their tops reach as high as a two-story house.

Scientists predicted every one of the bridge's support piers would encounter up to 6,000 ice ridges annually.[6] If the piers could not resist these impacts, the bridge would collapse. Gus Cammaert, scientist and author of *Ice Interaction with Offshore Structures*, was the primary ice consultant on the project. "I daresay that more effort was spent related to the ice engineering aspect of this bridge," he said, "than probably on any other [similar] structure that has ever been built."[7]

Research teams flew helicopters out to the floes to take ice core samples and measure weather conditions. This real-world data formed the basis of a computer model used to predict the bridge's response to ice collisions. The model included several different characteristics and behaviors of ice, including shape, strength, rate of growth, and speed of movement.

The breakthrough came when SCI engineers realized a different pier shape would make ice behave differently. If an ice floe struck a normal cylindrical bridge pier, it could push up against it and put a high load on the bridge structure. In contrast, if the ice were forced to travel up a slope, it would crumble under its own weight.

Using this principle, Giannelia's team designed bridge piers with a unique and complex shape. The base is a cone with a 52-degree angle.

Connected to this by a cylinder is another 52-degree cone extending across the waterline. Above this, a 78-degree cone meets the cylinder supporting the bridge girders. Called ice shields, the 52-degree cones cut through ice like a plow blade digging through soil.

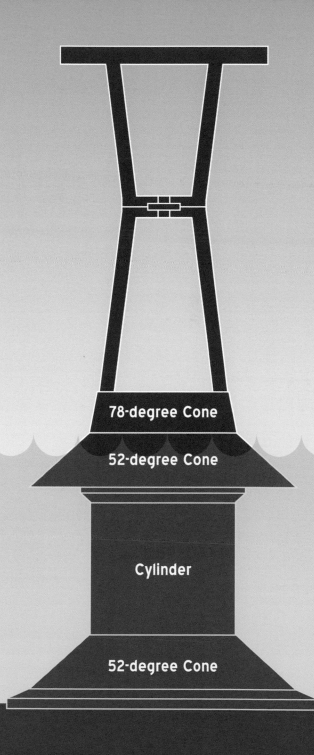

78-degree Cone

52-degree Cone

Cylinder

52-degree Cone

The cone shapes built into each pier help protect the bridge from ice damage.

CHAPTER 4

BRIDGING THE STRAIT

Typically, architects design structures, and engineers figure out how to build them. For Confederation Bridge, planning the construction methods was integral to the design process. After experiencing a winter blizzard on the Northumberland Strait, Paul Giannelia became convinced building over the water would not be safe or even possible. Instead, bridge elements would have to be constructed onshore and then transported to the site for installation.

"In my opinion, that was the single most important decision that was made," said Barry Lester, a structural engineer who worked on the

Innovative construction techniques were critical to the safe and successful completion of Confederation Bridge.

BEEFING UP THE BOAT

HLV *Svanen* is a large C-shaped vessel. Originally designed to build the smaller West Bridge in Denmark, it had to be modified to handle the heavy components used in the Northumberland Strait. Too big for most dry docks to handle, *Svanen* was floated onto a French beach on December 2, 1994—a day with exceptionally high tides. At low tide, a fleet of bulldozers built a dam behind the crane, allowing crews to rebuild it on dry land.

project. "It led directly to the way that this bridge was conceived and built."[1]

Because everything had to be moved, weight became the limiting factor. Individual bridge components had to be light enough that the Heavy Lift Vessel (HLV) *Svanen*, a floating crane, could handle them. No single piece could weigh more than 9,039 short tons (8,200 metric tons) or be lifted higher than 83 yards (76 m).[2]

With this in mind, engineers designed the bridge in three sections: a 0.8-mile (1.3 km) approach section over shallow water on the New Brunswick side, a 0.4-mile (0.6 km) approach on the Prince Edward Island side, and a 6.8-mile (11 km) main bridge over deep water in the strait.[3] On the central main bridge, 43 spans link 44 piers. Each span includes a 210-yard (192 m) girder weighing 8,267 short tons (7,500 metric tons).[4] Hinged spans are used to prevent a domino effect known as progressive collapse, in which one faulty section takes down the entire structure. In Confederation Bridge, a failing girder would simply drop out.

CASTING THE CONCRETE

To meet the 100-year life-span PWC required, SCI needed a material strong enough to handle loads and durable enough to withstand ice abrasion and corrosive seawater. Concrete was the logical choice. A mixture of gravel and glue-like cement, reinforced with a steel skeleton, concrete is poured wet and can harden into any shape.

The concrete for Confederation Bridge needed to be four to five times stronger than that used in sidewalks. This strength had never been achieved outside a lab before. To do it, SCI made several modifications to the standard mix. First, they replaced the normal gravel with specially manufactured cubic stones. This increased the stones' surface area, strengthening the bonds between them and the cement. Next

LIQUID ROCK

Completed by 125 CE, the dome of the Roman Pantheon is one of the oldest surviving concrete structures. Roman concrete included cement made of volcanic ash, lime, and water. Modern concrete uses Portland cement, patented by Joseph Aspdin in 1824. Supplementary cementitious materials (SCMs) such as fly ash and silica fume are needed to create high-performance concrete, with strength and durability that dramatically extend the life-span of a structure. As a bonus, SCMs are industrial by-products that would otherwise end up in landfills.

A monument dedicated to the construction crews in Borden, Prince Edward Island, is a replica of a cross section of the bridge.

they added fly ash, a residue created by burning coal, which increases strength. They also added silica fume, a powder made as a by-product of silicon production, which resists erosion and decreases permeability. Low permeability prevents chloride in seawater from seeping through the concrete and rusting the steel reinforcing bars within. The end result was a strong, durable concrete.

The bridge required a huge volume of concrete, most of which was poured at the casting yard in Borden. Maintaining a fast pace of production in winter brought unique challenges. When the hard components of concrete are mixed with water, the ensuing chemical reactions release a lot of heat. Steep temperature differences between the center of a piece and its surface can cause cracking, which compromises strength. To prevent this, pouring took place inside heated sheds.

Construction crews also found the cold conditions challenging. Project manager Harmen Blom, originally from Dutch company Ballast Nedham, said, "I was very impressed with the way the Canadian workers were able to work in the very cold conditions during the winter, and get the job done."[5]

PUTTING IT ALL TOGETHER

When components were ready for installation, sledges named *Turtle* and *Lobster* carried them from the casting yard to a jetty where *Svanen* could pick them up. The crane transported each piece to the growing bridge and lowered it into position. Like cord inside a beaded necklace, steel tendons pulled the concrete components together and held them in place. A single tendon contained between four and 31 cables, each one a

SURVEYING WITH SATELLITES

To ensure precise placement of bridge components, *Svanen* used the Global Positioning System (GPS). GPS units receive signals from orbiting satellites, calculating position based on the difference between the time the signal was sent and the time it was received.

When bridge design began in 1992, GPS was not accurate enough for the needs of the bridge builders. "So we started talking to the GPS gurus who were working on improved versions of the system," SCI surveying manager Mirek Bursa said. "We had to trust that developments would take place and the accuracy we needed would be there when we started placing components in the strait."[7] The gamble paid off. Using between eight and ten satellites for every placement, components were assembled with "absolute accuracy."[8]

seven-strand braid. The bridge contains 7,885 miles (12,690 km) of cable altogether.[6]

Svanen placed the first main girder on its pier on October 1, 1995. Only 24 main bridge pieces were installed that year. The remaining 151 were added between April and November of 1996. At 11:30 pm on November 19, 1996, *Svanen* placed the final piece—a drop-in girder between piers 34 and 35. The team lit fireworks to celebrate the success.

Tugboats pulled *Svanen* to the construction site.

That winter, construction crews worked on lighting and paving. They also installed the safety barrier flanking the bridge deck. Confederation Bridge opened on May 31, 1997, right on schedule.

Approximately 6,000 engineers, tradespeople, sailors, and scientists contributed to the design, testing, and construction of Confederation

ENVIRONMENTAL FACTORS

Confederation Bridge won the 1994 Environmental Achievement Award from the Canadian Construction Association for "the far-reaching and exhaustive environmental consideration" it embodied.[10] One of the biggest impacts was in fuel consumption. Each year, drivers on the bridge use less gasoline and emit less greenhouse gas than the ferry service the bridge replaced. Other environmental impacts included

- the creation of new waterfowl habitat on Prince Edward Island;

- the addition of a lighting system less likely to attract migrating birds than standard lighting;

- the installation of six osprey nesting platforms in the Cape Jourimain National Wildlife Area in the New Brunswick approach section; and

- the building of a new lobster habitat out of rocks excavated from the holes where the bridge piers are set.

Bridge, and the process fascinated the public.[9] More than 125,000 people toured the Borden casting yard, and engineers held hundreds of sessions to answer questions about the bridge. "I've never been on a project where everyone was so interested in how you do it," Kevin Pytyck recalled. He continued:

The interest among school children was unbelievable. . . . At the high school and university level they wanted to know all about our environmental policies, strategies, and management. Responding to this interest was a major project for us, but it would have been a missed opportunity if these young people hadn't had a chance to learn about the project while it was going on.[11]

It is likely this transparency helped build public acceptance for the project. At the party celebrating the bridge's completion, a triumphant Giannelia said, "Today is a day for professionals. Today is a day for champions. We are champions because we said we would do it, and we did it. We've got something out there in the strait that we can be very proud of."[12]

It was now possible to drive to Prince Edward Island in just 12 minutes at any time of year. More than a century after its first conception, engineers had made the fixed link a reality.

CHAPTER 5

REACHING FOR THE SKY

Thousands of miles southeast of Confederation Bridge is the desert city of Dubai, in the United Arab Emirates. This nation is made up of several emirates, territories ruled by monarchs known as emirs. Dubai is home to the Burj Khalifa. At 2,717 feet (828 m) tall, this enormous skyscraper broke new ground in civil engineering and shattered all previous records for height.[1]

Construction began on September 21, 2004, and the building opened on January 4, 2010. Completed at a cost of $1.5 billion, the Burj Khalifa is a 160-story vertical city containing apartments, offices, hotel

As workers started the Burj Khalifa's foundation, many other buildings were under construction in the growing city of Dubai.

RACE TO THE TOP

Daniel H. Burnham, designer of New York's Flatiron Building, once said: "Make no little plans. They have no magic to stir men's blood."[7]

Skyscrapers have been stirring the blood since 1884, when William Jenney built the ten-story Home Insurance Building in Chicago. Rapid advances in engineering soon sparked competition to build the world's tallest structure. The Burj Khalifa is the first Middle Eastern record holder in this category since the Great Pyramid.

suites, shops, restaurants, and even a library.[2] Built from 432,000 cubic yards (330,000 cu m) of concrete and enough steel reinforcing bars to go a quarter of the way around the world, the Burj took an international team 22 million person-hours to build.[3] Its developer, Emaar Properties, wanted a structure that would not only be the world's tallest, but would "stand as an example of humanity's highest aspirations."[4] To fulfill this vision, Emaar turned to famed Chicago engineering firm Skidmore, Owings & Merrill (SOM).

A SOLID FOUNDATION

SOM's first hurdle was to design a foundation that could support half a million short tons (450,000 metric tons) of concrete, glass, and steel—not an easy task in the sandy desert.[5] The construction site consisted of layered, flaky, fractured stone and sand. Workers had to drill 164 feet (50 m) down to find rock capable of supporting the foundation.[6]

Drilling through weak stone posed its own challenges. As drills were withdrawn from holes, the walls of the holes tended to collapse. To prevent this, engineers filled the holes with a slippery liquid called polymer slurry. Tony Kiefer, a geotechnical engineer who worked on the foundation, said, "The secret name for the contractors on-site is basically to call it 'snot.'"[8]

The "snot" exerted pressure on the walls, keeping the holes open until concrete could be poured on top. The dense concrete sank, displacing the slurry, which floated to the surface. The concrete then hardened to form the foundation's supporting piles. There are 194 piles beneath the Burj, each four feet (1.5 m) in diameter and 141 feet (43 m) long.[9] A reinforced concrete raft floats on top, distributing the building's weight across the piles in the same way a snowshoe spreads a person's bodyweight across a snowdrift. The foundation weighs 121,254 short tons (110,000 metric tons) all by itself.[10]

STANDING UP STRAIGHT

Soil is a mixture of air, water, and particles of different sizes and shapes. When loads are applied—such as the weight of a new building—particles pack together, forcing out air and water. Engineers call this settlement, and it is key to the stability of foundations.

The Leaning Tower of Pisa, for example, was built over two soil types that settled at different rates. The structure's famous tilt developed even before construction was finished. In contrast, when the Burj Khalifa reached 135 floors, settlement had distorted its foundation only approximately 1.2 inches (3 cm).[11]

The building's foundation was finished by March 2005.

Dubai's groundwater contains high concentrations of corrosive chloride and sulfates, and the foundation had to be durable enough to withstand their effects. Engineers added silica fume to the concrete to reduce the ability of water to seep through, but a cathodic protection system was also needed. This system prevented corrosion by running electricity through a titanium mesh next to the steel reinforcing bars. The presence of electricity prevents the formation of rust, which along with chloride and sulfates can weaken the bars.

ENGINEERING A SUPERSTRUCTURE

The Burj Khalifa's architect, Adrian Smith, believes a structure should suit its surroundings. "As the building rises from the ground," he said, "it wants to feel like it is being sculpted from the earth and crystallized into a vertical stalactite of glass and steel."[12] To achieve this effect in Dubai, Smith drew inspiration from a local three-petaled desert flower called *Hymenocallis*. The Burj's horizontal cross-section is Y shaped, and as its height increases, the points narrow, eventually leaving a single, central spire.

"The architects can conceive things to be built," Smith added. "But very rarely do they have the expertise for how to keep it up and build it in the most efficient ways. You need a team of structural engineers to do that."[13] SOM's William Baker led this team. It was his job to figure out how a building so tall and thin could actually stand up.

The solution was an innovative structural system Baker calls "the buttressed core." The Burj is composed of four pieces: one central, six-sided tower and three wings spaced evenly around the center.

Raised in the small town of Fulton, Missouri, William F. Baker loved physics and math classes as a student but did not know what he wanted to be when he grew up. "I took an aptitude test that told me I should consider engineering," he said. "I had to ask my mother what that was."[14]

In college, Baker took many science courses outside of the ordinary engineering curriculum. This experience allows him to work from basic scientific principles rather than simply building upon the structures of the past. After completing his master's degree in 1981, he got a job with SOM, where architecture and engineering go hand in hand. "In my opinion," Baker said, "this is why a high percentage of our designs are actually realized. We always think about how our buildings will be built as we design them."[15]

Baker has worked on dozens of structures around the world and holds several awards for innovative approaches to structural engineering. His specialty is supertall buildings, such as the Burj Khalifa and the 1,000-foot (300 m) twisted Cayan Tower, also in Dubai. Three of the four tallest buildings completed in 2009—including the Burj—were Baker's work.

Baker's twisting Cayan Tower is located just a few miles from the Burj Khalifa.

The buttressing wings push inward against the central core, holding it upright. The core, in turn, provides stiffness, anchoring the wings in place and preventing them from twisting.

Baker says a tall building is like a precision wristwatch—it will not function unless all the parts work together. Central walls extend from the core of the Burj to the tip of each wing. These walls mimic beams, providing horizontal resistance to the downward load exerted by gravity. Spaced along the height of the building, there are also five three-story groups of floors used for mechanical and maintenance purposes. From these, deep outrigger walls extend from the central core around the perimeter of the wings. The horizontal outriggers connect to vertical columns. This transfers lateral loads from the walls to the columns, which then channel them down to the foundation. The advantage of this system is increased efficiency.

ENGINEERING THE WIND

Gravity is the main source of vertical loads on a building. The most important lateral loads are caused by wind. Tall buildings can sway several feet in strong winds. This swaying can induce seasickness in a building's occupants. Extreme wind loads could even knock down a building.

The three-winged shape of the tower began to take shape as the building continued rising in 2006.

Because of the Burj's unprecedented height, existing guidelines for wind engineering were of limited use. The building had to be tested directly, using the wind tunnel lab at Rowan Williams Davies & Irwin (RWDI) in Guelph, Canada. Using climate and environmental data from the site and a 1:500 scale model of the tower, RWDI researchers tested the building's response to 36 different wind directions, at speeds up to 123 miles per hour (198 kmh).[16]

The results were shockingly bad. Predictions showed the initial design would sway much faster than recommended. Instead of giving up, however, Baker went back to work on the tower's design. First, he optimized the structure's internal engineering, so the gravity support system would also resist sideways motion. "It is comparable to spreading your feet to stabilize yourself in a strong wind," he said. "You are then able to use your own body weight to avoid toppling over."[17] Next, Baker

WINDS

Tall buildings create downdrafts that become strong horizontal winds, threatening the comfort and safety of pedestrians below. Engineers added wide pavilions to the Burj's base, providing a barrier to stop strong winds from forming. Balconies on the tower were a bigger challenge. After wind tunnel testing, engineers added divider screens and overhead trellises to reduce winds. Apartments are also equipped with wind-tracking panels that advise residents about conditions on their balconies. As a final safety feature, all balconies are fitted with flags to give occupants a visual indicator of wind speed.

realigned the structure so prevailing winds at the site would break against the outside edges of the wings, rather than striking with full force against the building's flat surfaces.

The final step involved what Baker calls "confusing the wind." On a skyscraper with flat sides, air rushes around the building, creating swirls of wind called vortices. Vortices traveling in the same direction combine, amplifying their strength. But because the Burj's wings change shape as the tower rises, wind striking the tower continually changes direction, scattering the vortices before they can strengthen.

The new and improved Burj was tested at RWDI to great success. Baker's team had slowed the tower's sway by approximately half, allowing the Burj to reach higher than engineers initially thought it could.

CHAPTER 6

LIFE AT THE TOP

Tens of thousands of residents, employees, and tourists occupy the Burj Khalifa at any given time. Keeping those people comfortable and safe was just as big an engineering challenge as keeping the building from falling down.

Climate control is among the most important considerations. Summer temperatures in Dubai reach 129 degrees Fahrenheit (54°C), and the building's glass and steel cladding is its first line of defense against this punishing heat.[1] Mounted in a framework of tracks, every panel interlocks with those surrounding it. The joints are weathertight

The Burj Khalifa's observation deck features huge windows that give visitors impressive views of Dubai.

COLLECTING CONDENSATION

Dubai's climate is both hot and very moist, averaging 90 percent humidity and sometimes reaching 98 percent.[3] The contrast between this warm, wet air and the cool interior of the building leads to condensation, which can discolor the Burj's cladding. Moisture buildup can even lead to electric shorts within the building.

One of the tower's environmentally friendly features is a collection system that captures condensation, storing it in holding tanks in the basement parking garage. This reclaimed water is used to water plants in the gardens surrounding the tower.[4]

yet flexible, so the cladding can expand and contract as external temperature varies.

Each panel is a sandwich of two glass sheets with a small air gap between them. The outer sheet can withstand high surface temperatures and is covered in a special coating that prevents light and solar heat from penetrating the building. The coating cannot block the infrared energy that radiates back from the hot desert sand, however. A different coating on the inner sheet of glass achieves this.

The Burj Khalifa's cladding contains approximately 28,000 individual panels. The panels come in several different sizes, but most are 4.5 feet (1.4 m) wide by 10.7 feet (3.3 m) high and weigh 800 pounds (360 kg).[2] After successful testing, the cladding phase of construction began in May 2007 and was completed in September 2009. Hundreds of engineers and technicians worked on this aspect of the project alone.

Despite the protective effect of the curtain wall, air conditioning is still needed to maintain comfortable temperatures inside the tower. Cool water runs through pipes from a central plant into the building, where it circulates through the air conditioners before exiting to be rechilled.

GOING UP

Skyscrapers would not exist without the elevator, a mid-1800s breakthrough in mechanical engineering. Even today's advanced elevators, however, cannot travel the entire height of the 163-floor Burj Khalifa.

To work around this limitation, engineers designed a transfer system similar to that pioneered in the original World Trade Center. The Burj Khalifa's nonstop express elevators take passengers to sky lobbies on floors 43, 76, and 123. These express cars hold 46 passengers each, travel 22 miles per hour (35 kmh), and reach floor 123 in less than 50 seconds.[5]

STACK EFFECT

In a wood-burning fireplace, smoke travels up the chimney because the hot air inside is lighter than the dense, cold air outside. This stack effect is reversed on the Burj Khalifa—heat outside the building causes the air-conditioned interior air to travel downward and out. Engineers controlled the stack effect by sealing passageways between floors to restrict airflow.

KEEPING CLEAN

Keeping the Burj's curtain wall free of desert dust posed an engineering problem all its own. The solution is nine window-washing machines parked inside the mechanical floors at levels 40, 73, and 109. Equipped with telescoping arms that reach both above and below, they travel around the building on 18 permanently mounted tracks.

GETTING OUT

When designing the Burj, engineers had to consider not only how people would live in it, but how they would escape it. How could thousands of occupants—including those with health issues or physical disabilities—safely evacuate during an emergency?

Part of the solution is emergency elevators known as lifeboats. Located in the building's structural core, lifeboats run on emergency power and are controlled by Dubai Civil Defense. Serving all the sky lobbies, they reduce evacuation time dramatically compared to using the stairs alone.

Engineers also adapted the tower's existing structural features to increase its safety in an emergency. Thick, reinforced concrete walls surround exit stairs and dedicated firefighter's elevators. These walls also enclose a radical new design feature: refuge rooms. Pressurized to keep out smoke and receiving clean air through fire-resistant pipes,

Maintenance workers regularly scale the entire height of the building, even reaching the pinnacle of the tower's spire.

refuge rooms can resist fire for up to two hours. Their purpose is to keep occupants safe while allowing emergency workers to control the pace of an evacuation.

BREAKING THE RECORD

The Burj Khalifa's engineers stretched construction technology to its limit, creating a structure that is both efficient and beautiful. When the tower opened in January 2010, the Council on Tall Buildings and Urban Habitat named it the tallest freestanding structure in the world, a record it still held in 2014.

Records, however, are made to be broken. Sometimes Baker is asked "Do you think someone will go taller?" He always replies, "I hope so!"[6]

THE NEXT WORLD'S TALLEST

In January 2012, work began on Kingdom Tower in Jeddah, Saudi Arabia. Designed by Adrian Smith, the architect behind the Burj Khalifa, Kingdom Tower will be at least 3,281 feet (1,000 m) tall, 568 feet (173 m) higher than the Burj.[7] The tallest building approved for construction as of 2014, Kingdom Tower was scheduled to open in 2019.

CHAPTER 7

UNITING THE WORLD

The Isthmus of Panama is a narrow ribbon of land connecting North and South America—a 40-mile (64 km) barrier dividing the Atlantic and Pacific Oceans. Explorers had dreamed of connecting the seas since the 1500s, but the task seemed impossible, especially after a French attempt to dig a canal in the late 1800s ended in failure and disgrace.

During the Spanish-American War (1898), a US warship spent two months completing the journey around the southern edge of South America, convincing future president Theodore Roosevelt building

French efforts to construct a canal in Panama were abandoned after more than a decade of work.

THE FRENCH CONNECTION

Between 1880 and 1888, Frenchman Ferdinand de Lesseps spearheaded the first attempt to build a canal in Panama. De Lesseps had overseen construction of Egypt's Suez Canal, and believed a similar design would work in Panama.

Engineer Godin de Lépinay disagreed. "At Suez there is a lack of water, the terrain is easy, the land nearly the same level as the sea," he said. "In [Panama], there is too much water, the terrain is mostly rock, the land has considerable relief, and finally the country is literally poisoned."[2]

De Lesseps ignored this advice at the cost of $287 million and the lives of more than 20,000 workers, most of whom died of disease.[3] The loss of money and workers led to the project's demise.

the Panama Canal was a matter of national security. In 1903, the United States supported Panama's rebellion against Colombia in exchange for ownership of a corridor through the heart of Panama's new country. In 1904, construction began under the motto The Land Divided—The World United.[1]

Chief Engineer John Findley Wallace was unprepared and overwhelmed, and the work floundered. Famed railroad engineer John Stevens replaced Wallace in 1905. Stevens's first impression of the project was dismal. "I believe I faced about as discouraging a proposition as was ever presented to a construction engineer," he said.

"I found no organization . . . no answerable head who could delegate authority . . . no cooperation existing between what might charitably be called the departments."[4] The Panamanian jungle was another serious obstacle—heavy rainfall rusted tools and provided a breeding ground for disease-bearing insects such as mosquitoes.

Despite Roosevelt's demand for progress, Stevens ordered all work to stop. He spent his first year assembling equipment, investing in construction infrastructure, and improving the workers' living conditions. A hands-on manager, Stevens walked the line, clambered up and down in the existing excavations, and asked endless questions. The answers convinced him the job could be done. "There is no element of mystery involved in it," Stevens said. "The problem is one of magnitude, not miracles."[5]

THE BIG DITCH

The Panama Canal would have three components. First, locks at the Atlantic and Pacific Oceans would raise and lower ships to the correct water level. Second, the Gatun Dam would create a reservoir that would fill the locks. Third, the Culebra Cut would be an eight-mile- (13 km) long channel dug through Panama's mountains.[6]

JOHN STEVENS

John Stevens was born in Maine on April 25, 1853. After training as a teacher, he became a surveyor for an engineering firm in 1874. For the next 31 years, Stevens located new railroad routes and supervised construction all over Canada and the United States. Much of the work took place in remote and dangerous territory.

When Roosevelt offered him the Panama Canal project in 1905, Stevens's first impulse was to refuse. Once committed, however, he revolutionized the project. Next to management skills, Stevens's ability to explain engineering concepts in plain language was his biggest contribution to the canal. At a government hearing, a senator asked whether the 100-foot- (30 m) high Gatun Dam could seriously be expected to hold back a 30-mile- (48 km) long lake. Stevens replied, "Well senator, earthen dikes of Holland hold back the Atlantic Ocean."[7]

After leaving Panama, Stevens built railroads in Siberia, Russia, and Manchuria, China, and was elected president of the American Society of Civil Engineers in 1927. Following his death in 1943, George Goethals said, "Stevens . . . was one of the greatest engineers who ever lived, and the Panama Canal is his greatest monument."[8]

BATTLING MOSQUITOES

One of the greatest challenges faced by the canal project was disease. The chief enemy in this struggle was the tiny mosquito. Dr. William Gorgas estimated that without intervention, 3,500 workers would die each year from mosquito-borne yellow fever and malaria.[11] With Stevens's support, Gorgas launched an extermination campaign—a daunting task in the enormous Canal Zone.

Gorgas's sanitation team fumigated buildings, spread oil on standing water to suffocate mosquito larvae, and purchased insect screens. Residents were even fined for every larva living in water near their homes.

The campaign was successful. On November 11, 1906, Gorgas gathered his doctors in the hospital autopsy room to see what he described as the last person to die of yellow fever in Panama.

This enormous hole in the ground was the largest engineering challenge Stevens faced. "Nothing but dogged determination and steady, persistent, intelligent work will ever accomplish the result," he said. "We are facing a proposition greater than was ever undertaken in the engineering history of the world."[9]

Stevens's approach was simple. First, workers blasted the mountainsides with dynamite. Then a fleet of steam shovels dug out the loosened rock and soil, five cubic yards (4 cu m) per scoop.[10] They loaded

Roosevelt, *center*, became the first sitting president to travel abroad during his visit to the Panama Canal work site.

it onto train cars to be hauled away by rail. Because digging began at the lower-elevation ends of the Culebra Cut and moved toward the high-altitude center, the heavily loaded trains traveled away downhill, saving time and fuel.

The railroad system acted like a giant conveyer belt, carrying away material from the site. As work progressed, however, the tracks constantly needed to be moved. Stevens invented a swinging machine that could lift and shift them without taking them apart, replacing the work of 400 men.

"They are eating steadily into the mountain cutting it down and down," President Roosevelt said after his famous visit to Panama in 1906.[12] In reality, the work was brutal. Between high temperatures and the shattering noise of dynamite and digging, Culebra Cut quickly earned the nickname "Hell's Gorge." More than 61 million pounds (28 million kg) of dynamite were used

RACISM AND THE PANAMA CANAL

Black West Indians supplied most of the unskilled labor used to build the canal. They were recruited with promises of wealth, but made extremely little money compared to the white US workers. Black workers did not receive sick leave or holidays, and they were assigned the most unpleasant and dangerous jobs. Of 138 accidental deaths classified as "violent" that occurred in the final year of construction, 106 were black workers.[13]

in the excavation. This was more explosive power than released in all previous US wars. Accidents were frequent. In the words of one West Indian worker, "The flesh of men flew in the air like birds many days."[14]

Landslides plagued the work site. The slope of the digging never reached the angle of repose, the tilt at which a slope stabilizes. As trenches deepened, landslides became common, tearing up track and burying equipment. When pressure built up inside the trench walls, they simply burst. Most unsettling were days when the base of the ditch actually rose, an effect caused by downward pressure exerted by the sides. Of the 110 million cubic yards (84 million cu m) of earth removed during excavations, 25 million cubic yards (19 million cu m) were due to landslides.[15]

THE GATUN DAM

When an exhausted Stevens resigned in 1907, George Washington Goethals of the US Army Corps of Engineers took over. "I found when I went to Panama," Goethals said, "that [Stevens's] organization was about as perfect as anyone could make it. The result was that more than half the work was done for me in advance."[16] The remaining half included completing the Culebra Cut, building the Gatun Dam, and constructing the locks.

The Gatun Dam contains approximately 30 million short tons (27 million metric tons) of packed soil and rock.

During the rainy season, Panama's Chagres River could rise 40 feet (12 m) in 24 hours.[17] This water would carry ships through the locks, but only if it could be controlled. Goethals built the Gatun Dam using soil from the Culebra Cut. In 1911, workers closed the spillway, preventing the

Chagres from emptying into the Atlantic Ocean. By 1914, Gatun Lake had reached its full depth.

The Gatun Dam supplied not only water but also electricity. It fed a hydroelectric plant that powered the locks. This was especially innovative at a time when most US houses did not have electricity.

THE LOCKS

Locks consist of large sets of watertight doors that separate a canal into sections. After a ship enters from one side, the doors are closed and the water level is equalized to that of the other side. Then the exit doors are opened and the ship continues on its way.

Construction on the Atlantic locks began on August 24, 1909. They consisted of three chambers, each 81 feet (25 m) deep, 110 feet (34 m) wide, and 1,000 feet (305 m) long.[18] The locks were broad enough to accommodate the *Titanic*, the largest commercial ship of the age. Engineers built a second set of chambers in parallel, creating two lanes of traffic with a shared central wall. The Pacific locks followed a similar design.

At that time, Panama's locks were the largest concrete structures ever built. Crews mixed concrete on the ground in buckets that held six short tons (5.4 metric tons). They hauled the buckets up towers flanking the locks, moving them into position using a system of cables. After the pour, workers spread the concrete by hand. The locks were built in 36-foot (11 m) sections, each taking a week to complete.[19]

Together, the Atlantic and Pacific locks contain 4.4 million cubic yards (3.4 million cu m) of concrete, seven times more than Confederation Bridge.[20] So much cement was needed that Goethals saved $50,000 by ordering workers to shake out empty bags before throwing them away.[21]

SAILING THROUGH A CONTINENT

On September 26, 1913, the first ship made a trial run through the Atlantic locks. It entered the lowest chamber and the double gates closed behind it, swinging shut like a saloon door. Built of steel plate riveted to an internal steel skeleton, each gate weighed approximately 59,000 short tons (53,524 metric tons).[22] Hollow inside, the gates floated in the water, dramatically reducing

FLOODING THE CUT

One of the last steps in canal construction was flooding the Culebra Cut. At 2:01 p.m. on October 10, 1913, President Woodrow Wilson pressed a button inside the White House. The signal traveled via telegraph to Panama, where a dike exploded at 2:02. As water poured into the trench, thousands of spectators let loose a roar of joy and relief.

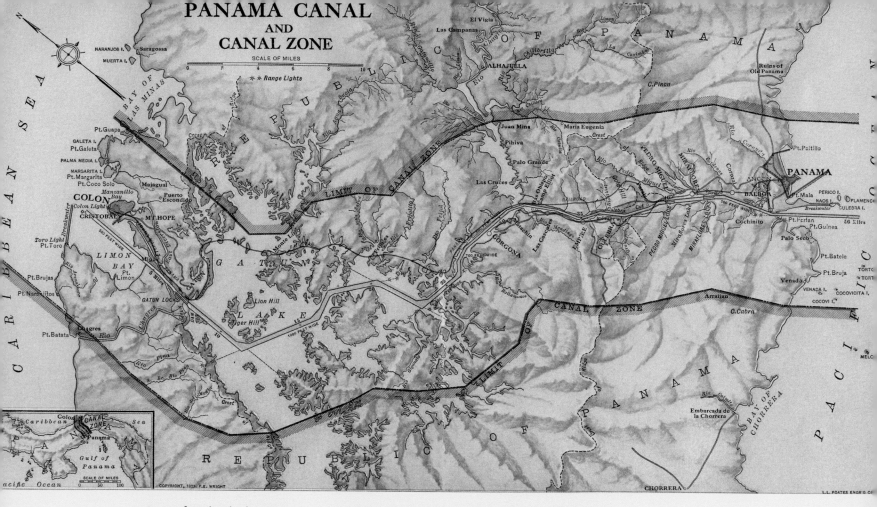

Once finished, the Panama Canal revolutionized transport in the Western Hemisphere.

the pressure on their hinges and making it possible to power them with a relatively small electric motor.

Once sealed, gravity-fed freshwater from Gatun Lake poured into the lock via culverts opening onto the chamber floor. Engineers controlled the flow using enormous valves. The sliding steel valves moved up and down like windows. When the chamber was full, the inner gates opened, admitting the ship to the higher central chamber.

The system worked flawlessly, and on August 15, 1914, the Panama Canal opened for business. More than 45,000 workers had contributed their labor, and 5,609 of them had died from accidents or disease.[23] The canal allowed ships to travel from ocean to ocean in hours rather than weeks or months.

"The creation of a water passage across Panama was one of the supreme human achievements of all time," wrote historian David McCullough, "the culmination of a heroic dream of four hundred years and of more than twenty years of phenomenal effort and sacrifice."[24] And while it changed the world forever, it seemed somehow inevitable. "A strange observer coming suddenly upon the scene would have thought that the canal had always been in operation," according to a passenger on the first commercial ship to traverse the canal.[25]

CHAPTER 8

GOING DEEP AND GETTING WIDE

The Panama Canal opened in 1914, but the engineering work was never truly completed. The number of ships that can pass through each day is limited by the availability of freshwater to fill the locks. In 1935, the US Army Corps of Engineers built a second reservoir to increase this availability, and in 2000, the Panama Canal Authority launched a project to deepen Gatun Lake.

In 1991, excavations began to widen the Culebra Cut. This increase allowed ships traveling in opposite directions to pass each other, rather than taking turns. These and other projects increased safety and

Expanding the canal requires enormous, powerful equipment.

reliability while allowing the canal to handle more traffic. There was still one major limitation, however: the size of the locks.

More than 1 million ships have traveled the canal since it opened.[1] Many were built specifically to fit the original locks, sliding through with inches to spare. By 2007, 27 percent of the world's sea cargo was carried in ships too big for the locks.[2] By 2013, half the ships in service or under construction simply would not fit.

On December 31, 1999, the United States transferred ownership of the canal to the Panamanian government. In a referendum held October 22, 2006, the Panamanian people voted in favor of a project to expand the canal for use by larger vessels. Work began September 3, 2007.

DIGGING DEEP

A ship's draft is the depth of water it needs to float without touching bottom. As cargo is added, weight increases, causing the ship to sink. The heavier the ship, the deeper the draft it requires. Deepening a channel by just one inch (2.54 cm) allows a ship to carry, for example, an extra 58,000 pairs of running shoes, worth $5 million.[3]

Ships built to the maximum size allowed by the original Panama Canal are known as Panamax ships. A Panamax ship can carry 4,500

Panamax ships were barely able to squeeze through the original locks.

cargo containers, while larger vessels can carry as many as 12,000.[4] To accommodate this increased size, Culebra Cut needed to be four feet (1.2 m) deeper.[5] Ships built to the new maximum size would be known as New Panamax ships. Engineers faced a challenge Stevens's crew did

RESCUE AND RESTORE

Before the jungle was cleared for excavation during the new expansion, wildlife rescue teams found and safely relocated frogs, turtles, crocodiles, snakes, sloths, birds, and other animals. For every acre of forest removed, two were reseeded with native trees. Workers planted hundreds of thousands of seedlings, including coastal mangrove forests.

Reforestation is not only good for the environment, but also for the functioning of the canal. The health of the surrounding forest influences rainfall and water flow throughout the area.

not—the excavation was underwater. Instead of being dug, the site would have to be dredged.

Engineers built a terrace three to five feet (1 to 1.5 m) above the water's surface. Hydraulic backhoes placed on the terrace could reach approximately 20 feet (6 m) down from that height to remove material from the water. Later, to break up rocky areas, engineers used drills mounted on barges. They inserted plastic tubes into the resulting holes and then packed them with dynamite. After blasting, bucket dredges scooped up the loosened rock; like giant vacuum cleaners, suction dredges pumped soft material up through steel pipes. The spoil was loaded on barges and carried away.

Dynamiting was the riskiest part of the process, because ships were allowed to pass through before and after it. Cargo ships cleared the bottom of the canal with just six feet (2 m) to spare, and if blasts deposited large boulders in the center of the passage, vessels would be delayed or even run aground. Engineers also deepened Gatun Lake to 89 feet (27 m), increasing capacity by 262 million cubic yards (200 million cu m) of water, enough for 1,100 extra ships per year.[6]

BIGGER, BETTER LOCKS

Sixty percent of the expansion project's budget was earmarked for construction of new locks. They would be able to accommodate ships 1,201 feet (366 m) long and 161 feet (49 m) wide, with a maximum draft of 49 feet (15 m).[7]

The new locks are made of high performance concrete containing gravel from the Pacific excavations. Their water culverts are big enough for two trains to pass side by side and can fill a chamber quickly using the locks' innovative water-saving basins.

The new gates gave engineers another chance to innovate. When repairs are needed, the 1914 swinging gates have to be removed and floated out to shipyards, shutting down a lane of traffic. In contrast,

PRESERVING THE PAST

The Panama Canal Authority partnered with the Smithsonian Tropical Research Institute to locate and study artifacts uncovered during expansion excavations. Discoveries include:

- Pre-Columbian arrowheads
- A dagger dating to 1590–1610 CE
- A brick waste incinerator built in 1908
- 3,485 fossils of various ancient species

the expansion gates are on rollers—in just five minutes, they slide open
perpendicular to the lock and can be fixed on-site. The first set of gates
arrived in August 2013. Designed for the middle lock chamber on the
Atlantic side, they are 189 feet (57.6 m) long, 33 feet (10 m) wide, and
99 feet (30.19 m) tall.[8] The lowest Pacific gate has to resist violent tides
and is the heaviest. Like the original gates, the new gates are hollow.

A NEW CENTURY FOR PANAMA

Planners intended to complete the expansion in 2014 for the canal's
one-hundredth anniversary. And since the expansion project began, ships
have continued increasing in size—Maersk Line, operator of the biggest
shipping fleet in the world, has ordered vessels that are too big even for
the new locks.

Alberto Alemán Zubieta, past administrator of the Panama Canal
Authority, believes the canal is still a unique asset to world shipping.
"There is still no other place in the world," he said, "where you could be in
another ocean in just a matter of hours."[9]

CHAPTER 9

ENGINEERING FOR THE FUTURE

Today and in the future, civil engineers face two major challenges: security and sustainability. The September 11, 2001, World Trade Center attacks brought security issues to the forefront. Engineers were among the first to study the site. They spent months trying to understand why impacts in one area of the towers caused the entire structures to crumble.

Engineers had planned for natural and manmade forces on the towers. The buildings were designed to withstand high wind loads or the impact of a Boeing 707 passenger jet. Still, no one expected much larger

The new tower at the World Trade Center site is designed to be safer and stronger than previous skyscrapers.

Boeing 767s to strike on a windy day. Since it is not possible to predict every type, magnitude, or combination of natural and unnatural loads a structure will experience, engineers are increasing safety by building to prevent the chain reactions known as progressive collapse.

The hinged girders on Confederation Bridge are one example of this. In addition, the United States Department of Defense (DOD) has conducted a series of blast experiments to study the movement of powerful, localized forces through models of government structures. While terrorism is the DOD's first concern, their results can also be applied to accidents, environmental forces, and general wear and tear. One promising solution supported by these tests is the alternate path method, which involves designing structures with multiple load-bearing pathways. That way, if one fails, a backup system can take on the added load and prevent collapse. This capability for a system to continue performing in the face of a disaster is known as resiliency.

But how far should these measures be taken? Ron Klemencic, past chairman of the Council on Tall Buildings and Urban Habitat, says,

If you think about it, there's a continuum between, say, a fire in a wastebasket and a meteor striking a building. Between those two events is a line that we have to draw and say, 'To the left of this line we will deal with from an engineering standpoint, but to the right of that line we are willing to take the risk.' And where is that line? That has to be a public decision.[1]

Engineers must communicate with architects, government officials, and the public to come to these conclusions.

SUSTAINABLE DEVELOPMENT

Worldwide, engineers are expanding the built environment at an incredible rate. A study by the Civil Engineer Research Foundation predicts that two-thirds of the future's thriving cities have not been built yet, that they will be built in developing nations, and that they will be the size of major cities that already exist in developed countries.

New advances in sustainable engineering will be needed to support this growth. The

ENGINEERS WITHOUT BORDERS

The international organization Engineers without Borders (EWB) partners skilled engineers with disadvantaged communities that need help developing basic infrastructure. Projects include everything from water supply and sanitation to energy and agriculture. All work is done with a focus on sustainability.

The US chapter of EWB has more than 13,800 members working on hundreds of projects around the globe every year. The chapter estimates that since 2002, their activities have improved the quality of life of 2.5 million people worldwide.[2] Many college students studying engineering participate in EWB projects.

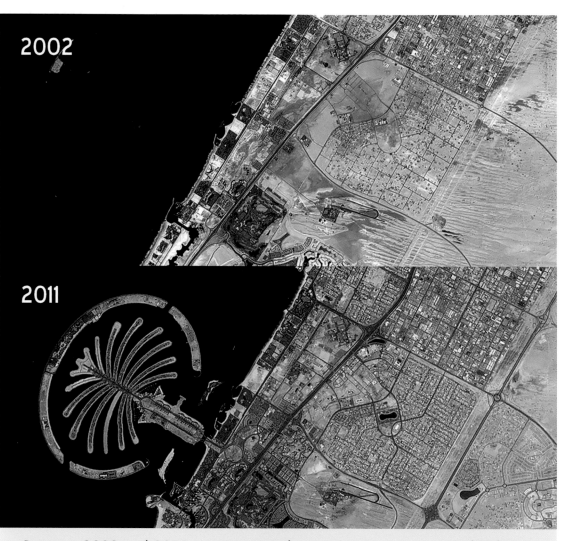

2002

2011

Between 2002 and 2011, enormous civil engineering projects turned Dubai into a major world city, complete with artificial islands and densely packed buildings. In these satellite photos, desert is tan, plant life is red, water is black, and buildings are silver.

American Society of Civil Engineers defines sustainable development as "the challenge of meeting human needs for natural resources, industrial products, energy, food, transportation, shelter, and effective waste management while conserving and protecting environmental quality and the natural resource base essential for future development."[3]

George Tamaro, designer of the World Trade Center's original foundations, says in the past, engineers have commonly been pressured to build as cheaply as possible. "But if there are subsequent problems . . . or if the structure doesn't last," he explained, "that costs more in the long run."[4] Today's engineers encourage their clients to consider life-cycle costs—the costs of building, inspecting, maintaining, and repairing a structure throughout its entire life-span. Some even consider budgeting for these costs to be an ethical responsibility inherent in the idea of sustainable development.

Another important goal for sustainability is to redirect the flow of resources. Today, many materials travel one way. Resources are harvested from the earth, infrastructure is built, and when the structure is decommissioned, its components are sent to the landfill. But what if the materials from outdated infrastructure could be reprocessed and repurposed for building new structures? According to Saeed Mirza, who specializes in infrastructure rehabilitation, "Implementation of the principles of sustainable development requires the engineer to reduce, reuse, recycle, and above all rethink."[5]

LEADING THE WAY

When asked to reflect on the future of his profession, civil engineer John Dionisio said:

> I think [it] will be even more important in the twenty-first century than it has been during the past two centuries. . . . Civil engineering touches just about every other engineering profession because you need to build the infrastructure that goes along with whatever it is. . . . So I think that if anyone is looking for a profession to get into, the message should be this is the one."[6]

Civil engineers have the potential to be more than master builders, however. They can be leaders of a global society. In 2012, British civil engineer Fred Durie wrote:

> Great human feats are achieved through advances in technology. . . . There is also, however, the human element, the spirit and the will to get things done, the confidence and creativity to take that imaginative leap, the sheer determination to prove the doubters wrong. Very often, the impossible is simply that which has not yet been achieved.[7]

HANDS-ON PROJECT
BUILDING A BRIDGE

People's safety in buildings and on bridges relies on how well civil engineers have done their jobs. Extensive testing and planning must be done long before construction begins to ensure a structure will be strong enough to do its job. Civil engineers often use models to carry out early testing on a new idea.

You can experience this testing process yourself by building a simple bridge out of drinking straws. You will need 20 straws, approximately three feet (1 m) of tape, and two piles of textbooks. Place the piles approximately ten inches (25 cm) apart. They will serve as the places the bridge will connect.

Engineers can look to past structures for ideas to incorporate into their new structures. Search the Internet for images of both real-life bridges and drinking-straw bridges. Then, based on what you have seen, sketch a plan for your own bridge. Build it out of the straws, using the tape to connect straws together.

Once your bridge is completed, spanning the two piles of textbooks, begin placing objects on the bridge to test its ability to hold weight.

Begin with small items, such as pennies. If the bridge holds, continue adding larger and larger objects until the structure fails. Pay careful attention to the way it collapses.

Finally, answer the following questions:

College engineering students create huge bridge models.

- Where did you draw inspiration for your bridge design? Does it look similar to any of the real-world bridges you looked at?

- What was your bridge holding when it collapsed?

- Based on the way your bridge collapsed, how might you change the design of a future bridge to make it hold more weight?

- Can you think of a way to simulate moving loads, such as the cars or people that move across a real bridge?

PLANNING A CAREER

Students interested in civil engineering should take math and science courses in junior high and high school to prepare for university admission. Group sports and extracurricular activities help build teamwork and leadership skills.

$\downarrow$

Once in college, students should take courses that involve lab and field work to get hands-on experience. Students can look for co-op programs, internships, and summer jobs in civil engineering to gain work experience prior to graduation. Engineering competitions are another way to gain experience in college.

$\downarrow$

Engineers interested in working in management or other leadership roles can work toward a graduate degree. Approximately one-fifth of practicing engineers have graduate degrees.

ESSENTIAL FACTS
CONFEDERATION BRIDGE

PROJECT DATES
The first proposal for a fixed link between Prince Edward Island and mainland Canada was made in 1885. Confederation Bridge opened on May 31, 1997.

KEY PLAYERS
Paul Giannelia and his engineering team, Strait Crossing Inc., won the contract to build Confederation Bridge. Gus Cammaert served as an ice consultant on the project.

KEY TOOLS AND TECHNOLOGIES
- Bridge components were cast from concrete on land and then transported to the site for installation by HLV *Svanen*, a floating crane.

- Builders used GPS to ensure accurate placement of all bridge components.

THE IMPACT OF CONFEDERATION BRIDGE
Design challenges included high safety requirements, a planned 100-year life-span, and ongoing concern about environmental impacts. Builders achieved these goals through innovative components and construction techniques, as well as special attention to environmental concerns. Confederation Bridge is now the longest bridge over ice-covered water in the world.

ESSENTIAL FACTS
BURJ KHALIFA

PROJECT DATES
Construction began on September 21, 2004, and the building opened on January 4, 2010.

KEY PLAYERS
The Burj Khalifa was designed by architect Adrian Smith and structural engineer William Baker of Chicago's Skidmore, Owings & Merrill (SOM).

KEY TOOLS AND TECHNOLOGIES

- To support the structure on unstable desert sand, geotechnical engineers used 194 concrete piles.

- To allow the Burj to withstand both vertical and lateral loads, William Baker designed a novel structural system he calls "the buttressed core."

THE IMPACT OF THE BURJ KHALIFA
When the building opened in January 2010, the Council on Tall Buildings and Urban Habitat named it the world's tallest freestanding structure. At 2,717 feet (828 m) and 160 stories tall, the Burj is the first Middle Eastern building to hold a height record since Egypt's Great Pyramid.

ESSENTIAL FACTS
PANAMA CANAL

PROJECT DATES
The United States began construction in 1904. The first trial lockage occurred on September 26, 1913, and the Panama Canal opened for business August 15, 1914. Under the Panamanian government and the Panama Canal Authority, the expansion of the canal began on September 3, 2007. It was expected to be complete in mid-2015.

KEY PLAYERS
John Findley Wallace served as the project's first chief engineer. In 1905, President Theodore Roosevelt replaced Wallace with railway engineer John Stevens.

KEY TOOLS AND TECHNOLOGIES
- Project leaders used innovative planning, organization, and construction infrastructure, including a highly efficient railroad system.

- Recent expansions and upgrades have introduced new rolling gates to the locks; unlike the old gates, they can be replaced on-site.

THE IMPACT OF THE PANAMA CANAL
One of the largest civil engineering projects in history, the Panama Canal achieved the centuries-old dream of connecting the Atlantic and Pacific Oceans. New expansions will open the canal to larger ships.

GLOSSARY

arch
A semicircular structure that bears weight while bridging a gap.

beam
Part of a building's structural system that is horizontal and bears the weight of roofs or stories above it.

buttress
A structural unit that transfers lateral loads down through supporting columns.

culvert
A covered channel used to transport water.

curtain wall
A building's surface that separates its interiors from the external environment without providing any structural support.

dredge
To excavate rock or dirt that is underwater.

ergonomics
The study of comfort and efficiency during a particular activity.

girder
A major supporting beam that spans the distance between two bridge piers.

infrastructure
The public structures and systems necessary for civilization.

lateral
In a sideways direction rather than up and down.

load
A force or weight applied to a structure.

outrigger
A beam or other structural element extending outward from the center of a building.

pier
A load-bearing column placed between two open spaces.

settlement
The compacting of soils after a new load is applied.

sledge
A vehicle mounted on runners used to carry loads over slippery or uneven terrain.

slide rule
A handheld mechanical device used to make calculations before the widespread use of digital calculators.

spoil
Unwanted rock and earth removed during excavation.

surveying
The process of precisely determining where a structure or component needs to be placed.

ADDITIONAL RESOURCES

SELECTED BIBLIOGRAPHY

Davidson, Frank, and Kathleen Lusk Brooke. *Building the World*. Westport, CT: Greenwood, 2006. Print.

Penn, Michael R., and Philip J. Parker. *Introduction to Infrastructure: An Introduction to Civil and Environmental Engineering*. Hoboken, NJ: Wiley, 2012. Print.

FURTHER READINGS

Engdahl, Sylvia. *Building the Panama Canal*. Detroit, MI: Greenhaven, 2012. Print.

Macaulay, David. *Built to Last*. Boston, MA: Houghton Mifflin, 2010. Print.

Oxlade, Chris. *Skyscrapers: Uncovering Technology*. Richmond Hill, ON: Firefly, 2006. Print.

WEBSITES

To learn more about Great Achievements in Engineering, visit **booklinks.abdopublishing.com**. These links are routinely monitored and updated to provide the most current information available.

FOR MORE INFORMATION

For more information on this subject, contact or visit the following organizations:

American Society of Civil Engineers (ASCE)

1801 Alexander Bell Drive

Reston, VA 20191

800-548-2723

http://www.asce.org

Founded in 1852, the ASCE is the oldest US engineering society. It advocates for advances in civil engineering, helps engineers further their careers, and promotes sustainability in engineering projects.

National Building Museum

401 F Street NW

Washington, DC 20001

202-272-2448

http://www.nbm.org

This museum features exhibits and information about the materials, structures, and spaces that make up the infrastructure of our modern world.

SOURCE NOTES

CHAPTER 1. WHAT IS CIVIL ENGINEERING?

1. *Big, Bigger, Biggest: Skyscraper*. Dir. Robert Hartel. National Geographic, 1 Apr. 2008. Television.

2. Ibid.

3. Ibid.

4. Anne Elizabeth Powell. "Celebrating the Greatest Profession." *Civil Engineering* 72.11/12 (2002): 235. Print.

5. Michael R. Penn and Philip J. Parker. *Introduction to Infrastructure: An Introduction to Civil and Environmental Engineering*. Hoboken, NJ: Wiley, 2012. Print. vii.

6. Anne Elizabeth Powell. "Celebrating the Greatest Profession." *Civil Engineering* 72.11/12 (2002): 236. Print.

7. "Civil Engineers." *Occupational Outlook Handbook*. Bureau of Labor Statistics, 8 Jan. 2014. Web. 27 Mar. 2014.

8. "Employment." *Civil Engineering*. Career Cornerstone Center, n.d. Web. 9 Dec. 2013.

9. "Civil Engineers." *Occupational Outlook Handbook*. Bureau of Labor Statistics, 8 Jan. 2014. Web. 27 Mar. 2014.

10. Jay Landers. "Leaders in Training." *Civil Engineering* 72.11/12 (2002): 248. Print.

11. Michael R. Penn and Philip J. Parker. *Introduction to Infrastructure: An Introduction to Civil and Environmental Engineering*. Hoboken, NJ: Wiley, 2012. Print. 156.

12. "2013 Report Card for America's Infrastructure." *American Society of Civil Engineers*. American Society of Civil Engineers, Mar. 2013. Web. 9 Dec. 2013.

13. Michael R. Penn and Philip J. Parker. *Introduction to Infrastructure: An Introduction to Civil and Environmental Engineering*. Hoboken, NJ: Wiley, 2012. Print. 6.

CHAPTER 2. BUILDING A PROFESSION

1. "Engineering." *Encyclopaedia Britannica*. Encyclopaedia Britannica, 2013. Web. 12 Dec. 2013.

2. Anne Elizabeth Powell. "Celebrating the Greatest Profession." *Civil Engineering* 72.11/12 (2002): 77. Print.

3. Frank Davidson and Kathleen Lusk Brooke. *Building the World*. Westport, CT: Greenwood, 2006. Print. 21.

4. Ibid. 22.

5. Henry Petroski. *The Essential Engineer: Why Science Alone Will Not Solve Our Global Problems*. New York: Knopf, 2010. Print. 20.

6. Anne Elizabeth Powell. "Considering the Future of the Profession." *Civil Engineering* 72.11/12 (2002): 232. Print.

7. Michael R. Penn and Philip J. Parker. *Introduction to Infrastructure: An Introduction to Civil and Environmental Engineering*. Hoboken, NJ: Wiley, 2012. Print. 13.

8. P. A. Johnson. "State of Women in Civil Engineering in the United States and the Role of ASCE." *Journal of Professional Issues in Engineering Education and Practice* 139.4 (2013): 275. Print.

9. Ibid. 279.

10. Sarah Buck. "Women Reach the Top in Civil and Structural Engineering." *Proceedings of the Institution of Civil Engineers-Civil Engineering* 161.1 (2008): 9. Print.

11. Mike Chrimes and Amar Bhogal. "Civil Engineering—A Brief History of the Profession: The Perspective of the Institution of Civil Engineers." *International Engineering History and Heritage*. Reston, VA: American Society of Civil Engineers, 2001. Print. 73.

12. Ibid. 90.

CHAPTER 3. A FIXED LINK

1. I. A. Brookes. "Northumberland Strait." *Historica Canada*. Historica Canada, 24 Jan. 2014. Web. 27 Mar. 2014.

2. Copthorne MacDonald. *Bridging the Strait: The Story of the Confederation Bridge Project*. Toronto, ON: Dundurn, 1997. Print. 47.

3. Ibid. 40.

4. Ibid. 50.

5. Harry Thurston. *Building the Bridge to P.E.I.* Halifax, NS: Nimbus, 1998. Print. 7.

6. T. G. Brown, et al. "Extreme Ice Load Events on the Confederation Bridge." *Cold Regions Science and Technology* 60.1 (2010): 1. Print.

7. Harry Thurston. "Strait Across." *Canadian Geographic* 117.2 (1997). Web. 2 Dec. 2013.

CHAPTER 4. BRIDGING THE STRAIT

1. Copthorne MacDonald. *Bridging the Strait: The Story of the Confederation Bridge Project*. Toronto, ON: Dundurn, 1997. Print. 42.

2. "HVL Svanen." *Ballast Nedham*. Ballast Nedham, n.d. Web. 16 Dec. 2013.

3. Copthorne MacDonald. *Bridging the Strait: The Story of the Confederation Bridge Project*. Toronto, ON: Dundurn, 1997. Print. 59.

4. Harry Thurston. *Building the Bridge to P.E.I.* Halifax, NS: Nimbus, 1998. Print. 26.

5. Copthorne MacDonald. *Bridging the Strait: The Story of the Confederation Bridge Project*. Toronto, ON: Dundurn, 1997. Print. 99.

6. Ibid. 112.

7. Ibid. 84.

8. Jim Wilson. "GPS Helps to Build a Bridge." *Popular Mechanics*. Popular Mechanics, Oct. 1997. Web. 27 Mar. 2014.

9. Harry Thurston. *Building the Bridge to P.E.I.* Halifax, NS: Nimbus, 1998. Print. 47.

10. Copthorne MacDonald. *Bridging the Strait: The Story of the Confederation Bridge Project*. Toronto, ON: Dundurn, 1997. Print. 73.

11. Ibid. 120.

12. Ibid. 108.

CHAPTER 5. REACHING FOR THE SKY

1. "The Tower." *Burj Khalifa*. Burj Khalifa, 2013. Web. 9 Dec. 2013.

2. Blair Kamin. *Terror and Wonder: Architecture in a Tumultuous Age*. Chicago, IL: U of Chicago P, 2010. Print. 123.

3. "The Tower." *Burj Khalifa*. Burj Khalifa, 2013. Web. 9 Dec. 2013.

4. Peter A. Weismantle, Gregory L. Smith, and Mohamed Sheriff. "Burj Dubai: An Architectural Technical Design Case Study." *The Structural Design of Tall and Special Buildings* 16 (2007): 335. Print.

5. *Big, Bigger, Biggest: Skyscraper*. Dir. Robert Hartel. National Geographic, 1 Apr. 2008. Television.

6. Ibid.

7. Isabel Kuhl. *Architecture: The Groundbreaking Moments*. New York: Prestel, 2012. Print. 119.

8. *Big, Bigger, Biggest: Skyscraper*. Dir. Robert Hartel. National Geographic, 1 Apr. 2008. Television.

9. W. F. Baker, D. S. Korista, and L. C. Novak. "Burj Dubai: Engineering the World's Tallest Building." *Structural Design of Tall and Special Buildings* 16.4 (2007): 366. Print.

10. Ibid. 367.

11. "The Tower." *Burj Khalifa*. Burj Khalifa, 2013. Web. 9 Dec. 2013.

SOURCE NOTES CONTINUED

12. Adrian Smith. "Burj Dubai: Designing the World's Tallest." *CTBUH 8th World Congress, Dubai. March 3–5, 2008*. Dubai: Council on Tall Buildings and Urban Habitat, 2008. Print. 2.

13. Blair Kamin. *Terror and Wonder: Architecture in a Tumultuous Age*. Chicago, IL: U of Chicago P, 2010. Print. 112.

14. W. F. Baker. "Engineering an Idea: The Realization of the Burj Khalifa." *Civil Engineering* 80.3 (2010): 44. Print.

15. Ibid. 46.

16. Peter A. Irwin and William F. Baker. "The Burj Dubai Tower: Wind Engineering." *Structure Magazine* June 2006: 28. Print.

17. W. F. Baker. "Engineering an Idea: The Realization of the Burj Khalifa." *Civil Engineering* 80.3 (2010): 47. Print.

CHAPTER 6. LIFE AT THE TOP

1. Peter A. Weismantle, Gregory L. Smith, and Mohamed Sheriff. "Burj Dubai: An Architectural Technical Design Case Study." *The Structural Design of Tall and Special Buildings* 16 (2007): 353. Print.

2. G. F. Shapiro. "Burj Khalifa Curtain Wall." *Architect* 99.3 (2010): 24. Print.

3. Carly Fordred. "A Tall Order - Cooling Dubai's Burj Khalifa." *HVAC&R Nation* 2010: 11. Print.

4. "The Tower." *Burj Khalifa*. Burj Khalifa, 2013. Web. 9 Dec. 2013.

5. *Big, Bigger, Biggest: Skyscraper*. Dir. Robert Hartel. National Geographic, 1 Apr. 2008. Television.

6. W. F. Baker. "Engineering an Idea: The Realization of the Burj Khalifa." *Civil Engineering* 80.3 (2010): 47. Print.

7. "Interesting Facts About Kingdom Tower." *Kingdom Tower Skyscraper*. n.d. Web. 9 Dec. 2013.

CHAPTER 7. UNITING THE WORLD

1. David McCullough. *The Path between the Seas: The Creation of the Panama Canal 1970–1914*. New York: Simon, 1977. Print. 481.

2. Ibid. 80.

3. Ibid. 235.

4. Ibid. 462–463.

5. *American Experience: Panama Canal*. Dir. Stephen Ives. PBS. 24 Jan. 2011. Television.

6. "Gaillard Cut." *Encyclopaedia Britannica*. Encyclopaedia Britannica, 2014. Web. 27 Mar. 2014.

7. Cliff Schexnayder. "John F. Stevens—a Great Civil Engineer." *Journal of Construction Engineering & Management* 126.5 (2000): 329. Print.

8. Ibid.

9. David McCullough. *The Path between the Seas*. New York: Simon, 1977. Print. 480.

10. Ibid. 496–497.

11. Noel Maurer and Carlos Yu. *The Big Ditch*. Princeton, NJ: Princeton U P, 2011. Print. 123.

12. David McCullough. *The Path between the Seas*. New York: Simon, 1977. Print. 498.

13. Ibid. 582.

14. Ibid. 546.

15. Noel Maurer and Carlos Yu. *The Big Ditch*. Princeton, NJ: Princeton U P, 2011. Print. 103.

16. Cliff Schexnayder. "John F. Stevens—a Great Civil Engineer." *Journal of Construction Engineering & Management* 126.5 (2000): 325. Print.

17. *A Man, a Plan, a Canal, Panama*. Dir. Carl Charlson. NOVA, 3 Nov. 1987. Television.

18. David McCullough. *The Path between the Seas*. New York: Simon, 1977. Print. 590.

19. Ibid. 593.

20. Ibid. 592.

21. Ibid. 594.

22. Noel Maurer and Carlos Yu. *The Big Ditch*. Princeton, NJ: Princeton U P, 2011. Print. 103.

23. David McCullough. *The Path between the Seas*. New York: Simon, 1977. Print. 559.

24. Ibid. 613.

25. Ibid. 609.

CHAPTER 8. GOING DEEP AND GETTING WIDE

1. Michael R. Penn and Philip J. Parker. *Introduction to Infrastructure: An Introduction to Civil and Environmental Engineering*. Hoboken, NJ: Wiley, 2012. Print. 144.

2. Robert L. Reid. "Panama Plans to Expand Canal with Larger Locks." *Civil Engineering* 77.1 (2007): 14. Print.

3. National Ocean Service. "An Inch of Water: What's It Worth?" *Features*. National Oceanic and Atmospheric Administration, n.d. Web. 3 Jan. 2014.

4. "Modernization of the Panama Canal." *Washington Post*. Washington Post, 13 Jan. 2013. Web. 27 Mar. 2014.

5. "Panama Canal Expansion Program 2010 (Part 1)." *ACP*. ACP, 2010. Web. 27 Mar. 2014.

6. "Panama Canal Expansion Program September 2013." *ACP*. ACP, 2013. Web. 27 Mar. 2014.

7. Robert L. Reid. "Panama Plans to Expand Canal with Larger Locks." *Civil Engineering* 77.1 (2007): 13. Print.

8. "Panama Canal Expansion Program September 2013." *ACP*. ACP, 2013. Web. 27 Mar. 2014.

9. Andres Schipani and Robert Wright. "Panama Canal: Out of the Narrows." *Financial Times*. Financial Times, 25 Aug. 2013. Web. 16 Dec. 2013.

CHAPTER 9. ENGINEERING FOR THE FUTURE

1. Jay Landers and Laurie A. Shuster. "Progressive Wisdom." *Civil Engineering* 72.11/12 (2002): 187. Print.

2. "Our History." *Our Story*. Engineers Without Borders USA, n.d. Web. 10 Dec. 2013.

3. Richard H. McCuen, Edna Z. Ezzell, and Melanie K. Wong. *Fundamentals of Civil Engineering: An Introduction to the ASCE Body of Knowledge*. Boca Raton, FL: CRC, 2011. Print. 44.

4. Jay Landers and Laurie A. Shuster. "Progressive Wisdom." *Civil Engineering* 72.11/12 (2002): 181. Print.

5. S. Mirza. "Durability and Sustainability of Infrastructure—a State-of-the-Art Report." *Canadian Journal of Civil Engineering* 33.6 (2006): 646. Print.

6. Anne Elizabeth Powell. "Considering the Future of the Profession." *Civil Engineering* 72.11/12 (2002): 243. Print.

7. Fred Durie. "Burj Khalifa: Creating the World's Tallest Integrated 'Vertical City.'" *CTBUH Shanghai Congress 2012—Asia Ascending: Age of the Sustainable Skyscraper City*. 2012. Print. 79.

INDEX

ABOUT THE AUTHOR

L. E. Carmichael never outgrew that stage of childhood when nothing is more fun than amazing your friends with your stockpile of weird and wonderful facts. Since completing her PhD, she has written children's books about everything from animal migration to hybrid cars. Based in Nova Scotia, Canada, Carmichael has taken the former Prince Edward Island ferry and driven over Confederation Bridge.

ABOUT THE CONTENT CONSULTANT

David A. Lange was drawn to civil engineering by wonderful and amazing structures such as the ones discussed in this book. He has taught civil engineering classes at the University of Illinois for more than 20 years, and he leads a research group that studies concrete materials for pavement, railroad, and airport infrastructure. Lange has conducted experiments on Illinois bridges, Canadian railroads, and runways at O'Hare International Airport in Chicago.